CLYDESDALE
IN OLD PHOTOGRAPHS

SPRING PLOUGHING at Dunsyre.

CLYDESDALE
IN OLD PHOTOGRAPHS

COLLECTED BY
LESMAHAGOW PARISH
HISTORICAL ASSOCIATION

ALAN SUTTON

Alan Sutton Publishing Limited
Phoenix Mill · Far Thrupp · Stroud · Gloucestershire

First Published 1991

British Library Cataloguing in Publication Data

Clydesdale in old photographs.
I. Lesmahagow Parish Historical Association
941.469

ISBN 0-7509-0050-4

Typeset in 9/10 Korinna.
Typesetting and origination by
Alan Sutton Publishing Limited.
Printed in Great Britain by
The Bath Press, Avon.

CONTENTS

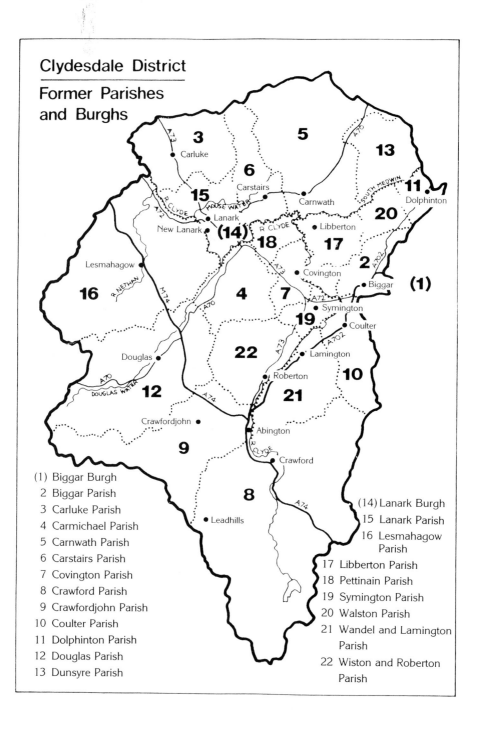

Clydesdale District

Former Parishes and Burghs

3 Carluke

5

13

6 Carstairs

15 Carnwath

11 Dolphinton

20

Lanark

New Lanark **(14)** Libberton

18 **17**

2

Lesmahagow Covington Biggar **(1)**

16 **4** **7** Symington

19 Coulter

22 Lamington

Douglas **10**

12 Roberton

Crawfordjohn **21**

Abington

9

Crawford

8

Leadhills

(1) Biggar Burgh
2 Biggar Parish
3 Carluke Parish
4 Carmichael Parish
5 Carnwath Parish
6 Carstairs Parish
7 Covington Parish
8 Crawford Parish
9 Crawfordjohn Parish
10 Coulter Parish
11 Dolphinton Parish
12 Douglas Parish
13 Dunsyre Parish

(14) Lanark Burgh
15 Lanark Parish
16 Lesmahagow Parish
17 Libberton Parish
18 Pettinain Parish
19 Symington Parish
20 Walston Parish
21 Wandel and Lamington Parish
22 Wiston and Roberton Parish

INTRODUCTION

Although Lanarkshire is one of the most highly industrialized and densely populated parts of Scotland, the old political divisions of Nether and Upper Wards nicely demarcate the more industrial and the more rural parts of the county. During the last century and a half the increasing population in the north of the county has led to the division of Nether Ward into Lower and Middle, but Upper Ward has remained largely the same and includes the parishes of Biggar, Carluke, Carmichael, Carnwath, Carstairs, Covington, Culter, Crawford, Crawfordjohn, Dolphinton, Douglas, Dunsyre, Lanark, Lesmahagow, Liberton, Pettinain, Symington, Walston, Wandell and Lamington, and Wiston and Roberton (nineteenth-century spellings). This is closely co-extensive with the modern Clydesdale District.

If Clydesdale has not played a continuously important part in Scotland's history, it has been the cradle of more than one decisive episode. The Wallace raised his standard in Lanark, and the political and religious fate of Scotland was effectively sealed by the actions of the Covenanters in the seventeenth century.

The rapid industrialization of Britain did not spare this corner of Scotland although it was essentially rural in nature. Mining for ironstone laid waste large tracts in the north-east. Villages like Lesmahagow and Coalburn prospered and fared ill as the coal industry waxed and waned. The home-based spinning and weaving industries of the eighteenth century quickly became industrialized in places like New Lanark as new power sources were utilized. But these too declined with the import of cheap synthetics from abroad. Indeed the wheels of industry have turned full circle, so that Clydesdale is once again largely rural, and the villages have expanded to accommodate commuters to Glasgow who prefer to live in more peaceful surroundings.

Clydesdale remains most famous for its fruit growing, an industry which goes back to the monks of Kelso, who had the abbey at Lesmahagow. Change is evident here too: the ubiquity of the family fruit garden has given way in the face of changes in agricultural practice and the constant demand for building land. The market gardens of the Clyde Valley now cater for the gardener as much as the greengrocer.

L.P. Hartley said, 'The past is a foreign country: they do things differently there', but, though the methods may have changed, the concerns of our fathers and grandfathers are similar to ours. Our cars may go faster than theirs, but the rail network laid down by the Victorian entrepreneurs has almost gone; the worm who 'forgives the plough' may not forgive the tractor; what is left of Lesmahagow coal, once the finest for gas production, is sold to fire Northern Ireland's power stations. Our smallest communities strive to maintain an independence in the face of increasing pressures for a bland uniformity.

Clydesdale is a very large area and, because of this, we have chosen to group our photographs by district, with groups of parishes lumped together, rather than by activity. Inevitably some of the less populous parishes have thrown up only a few photographs, but we have done our best to provide a wide coverage, although the larger burghs and parishes provide the lion's share.

The members of the Lesmahagow Parish Historical Association would wish to thank the following for the loan of photographs and for information: Clydesdale District Libraries and Information Service; Carluke Parish Historical Association; Dr Ken Liddell; Anna Shearer; New Lanark Conservation Trust; Derek Bates; George Paul; Brian Lambie; Bill Muir; Nic Broadbridge; John Hunter.

Biggar and District

East End, Biggar

EAST END, BIGGAR, about 1905. Now a busy corner, with the police station off to the left. The background houses made way for the Jubilee Garage in 1935.

THE CADGER'S BRIG was the main Glasgow road until superseded by the new road and bridge to the right in 1823. William Wallace crossed over it, disguised as a cadger (itinerant hawker), in 1296, seeking out the English forces prior to the battle of Biggar.

CADGER'S BRIG about twenty years later. The wheels of the gasholder can just be made out in the centre background. The town gasworks is possibly the only one remaining in Scotland and is now a museum.

BIGGAR, shortly after 1900. Most of these buildings remain the same, but it is now a bit more difficult to cross the A702 trunk road. The old school (in the middle distance) is now in the town hall.

BIGGAR MILL. Little has changed here except for the addition of Greenhill Farmhouse, transported here from Wiston by Biggar Museum Trust as a Covenanters' museum in 1986. Note the sheep being herded along the road to the right.

BIGGAR FOUNTAIN commemorated Queen Victoria's Jubilee in 1887. It survived the Second World War only to be scrapped in 1947 by the town council. Luckily, one local lady rescued the four little boys on dolphins and they now adorn her garden.

THE VICTORIANIZED MANSE of the old United Presbyterian church, c. 1910, where the essayist Dr John Brown was born in 1810. It was much altered in the 1980s when many internal features were destroyed and larger windows and a porch inserted.

BIGGAR HIGH STREET with the Clydesdale Hotel advertising a motor garage. Behind the railings is the Gillespie Kirk, now the Gillespie Centre, while the house on the extreme right is an Abbeyfield Home.

THANKERTON in 1915. Bicycles were clearly all the rage.

A VIEW OF THANKERTON in about 1905, from the wooden railway footbridge.

THANKERTON VILLAGE showing the footbridge over the main line. In 1847 the railway from Carlisle to Glasgow cut the village in half. A road bridge was built some distance up the brae, but only the footbridge marked the old right of way. It was removed when the station closed.

CENTRAL THANKERTON in about 1913. The thatched cottage on the right has been replaced by a modern bungalow.

THE RAILWAY STATION AT TOWNHEAD, THANKERTON about 1910. Though closed, the station still exists, fenced off from the London trains by a tall wire fence.

SYMINGTON SCHOOL AND SCHOOLHOUSE in about 1907. The replacement for this school is itself about to be replaced.

THE TINTO HOTEL (named for the local mountain, 2,300 ft) shortly after opening in October 1914. Now greatly extended, the hotel still has a fine stained glass window on the stair landing illustrating the verse: *Be a lassie ne'er sae black, / If she has the penny sillar, / Set her up on Tinto tap / The wind'll blaw a man until her.*

COULTER VILLAGE in 1905. The cottages were renovated in 1870, and have been skilfully modernized again in the 1960s.

COULTER, MILL COTTAGE. The mill off to the left has been converted into a roadside restaurant.

SYMINGTON, TOWNFOOT in about 1903. The old thatched library on the right was replaced by council housing in the 1930s.

MAJOR TELFER BUILT THIS LITTLE FOLLY, seen here in about 1907, on his Symington Lodge Estate. It is now slated and contains all mod. cons. The major himself is buried a few hundred yards away on the banks of the Clyde – to give him a head start on the Day of Judgement, it is said.

COVINGTON in about 1910, with the village school on the right.

NEWTON OF COVINGTON with Quothquan Law in the background. The houses on the left still exist, some slated, some still with thatch under corrugated iron.

THE GREEN AT SKIRLING in 1930, just over the border in Peeblesshire. This was the scene of many large fairs up until 1867, when they were transferred to neighbouring Biggar.

SKIRLING as it appeared at the turn of the century.

LAMINGTON ESTATE VILLAGE was entirely rebuilt during the ownership of the first Baron Lamington (1838–90) and is now a conservation area of outstanding importance. It is seen here in about 1904.

LAMINGTON GLEN was laid out by the first Baron Lamington more than a century ago, with many trees planted by royalty and parliamentary visitors. Cleared in 1949, it has now returned to its former glory. The 'haystack' was a bathing hut built for Annabella, Lady Lamington.

A SCENE AT WISTON, not much changed today, although the shop has ceased to do business. The wall-mounted letter box has been made famous by a recent postcard producer.

WISTON MILL & MARSHLANDS.

WISTON MILL is now a private house, the fate of many of the surviving mills in the area.

GENERAL VIEW OF ROBERTON in 1904. The old school on the right is now the village hall.

Roberton from Linn Knowe

LAMINGTON MILL (left foreground) was used as the village hall in the 1930s; it is now a private residence, as is the church in the background. The scene here dates from about 1907.

MARYWELL, COULTER.

COULTER, TOWNFOOT in about 1912. Marywell is the name of the nearest house in this view. The entrance to Cornhill Old People's Home is on the right at the foot of the hill.

DOLPHINTON, 1904, looking east from the hamlet, and showing a horse with his head in a nosebag, and a baker's cart. Hamlets and isolated houses were dependent on supplies being brought by horse and van.

Carluke and the Clyde Valley Villages

HIGH STREET in the early 1900s. The thatched building on the left is the 'Wee Thackit' public house, now sadly minus its eponymous roof. The elaborate lamp post was the traditional gathering place at Hogmanay. The 1715 bell-tower can just be seen at the bottom left of the street.

THE RANKIN MEMORIAL HALL AND LIBRARY was built by public subscription in 1884 in memory of Dr Daniel Reid Rankin. Rankin was a well-loved and much respected figure in the town. A doctor of medicine, he also contributed greatly to Scottish geological knowledge. His book *Notices Historical, statistical and biographical, relating to the Parish of Carluke from 1288 to 1874*, is still today a valuable source of information on Carluke's past.

THE PLAYING FIELD behind the Crown Hotel is known as the 'Wee Moss'. The wooden building in the background housed St Athanasius' Primary School until a new school building was erected in the 1970s. Carluke fire station was later built in the playground area.

A VIEW OF CHAPEL STREET in around 1900. The shop on the right is Johnny Morton's. The buildings on the right-hand side of the photograph were demolished in the late 1970s when a new road system was built.

ONE OF THE GREAT CHARACTERS of Carluke, still remembered by some of the older inhabitants, was 'Punkie Willie', otherwise Willie Ewings. He was a chimney sweep and also acted as town crier.

THE HIGH MILL stands at the top of Chapel Street. The mill tower was built about 1797 by David Dick who was appointed baron baillie of Carluke in 1815. Dick's sons converted the mill to steam power and the family tradition of milling continued into the early twentieth century. The mill fell into disuse about 1930. The High Mill was chosen as the logo of the Carluke Parish Historical Society in 1980, and has recently been acquired by the High Mill Trust who have begun to renovate this unique building.

CARLUKE CROSS in around 1906. The main Carlisle to Stirling road which runs through the centre of the picture was built as a turnpike road in 1823.

THE MILK CART WITH ITS CHURNS was a common sight around the town. It came round twice daily after the milking. Customers took their own jugs out to the cart to have them filled from the tap on the churn.

Market Place School, Carluke.

MARKET PLACE SCHOOL, or Carluke Higher Grade as it became, was erected in 1876. The bell from the school tower was restored and now stands in the new High School, Carnwath Road.

LANARK ROAD. The bridge was called Stark's Bridge locally. Andrew Stark founded the Burnside Sawmills, the entrance to which was to the right of the photograph.

THE BOTTOM OF THE HIGH STREET in around 1900. The thatched, whitewashed shop on the left was Gunn's fish shop. The group of people on the right are standing outside the Black Bull Inn, which dates from the 1790s; one of the oldest buildings in the town, it retains its name to the present day.

CROSSFORD VILLAGE lies in three parishes: Lesmahagow, Lanark and Carluke. Crossford Bridge was built in 1852. It stands about 100 yd above the original ford on the old road to Lanark.

THE TOWER AND FORTALICE OF BRAID-WOOD, or Halbar Tower as it is known locally, stands on the steep braes between Braidwood and Crossford. It is not known how old the tower is but it is certainly mentioned in an Act of 1581.

THE LAIGH, OR LOW, MILL IN CARLUKE was a water-mill which stood on the Minister's Burn near to Stark's Bridge on the present Lanark Road. It was used until 1940, grinding peanuts for oil during the Second World War. The mill buildings no longer exist.

STRAWBERRY PICKING was, and still is, a seasonal job around Carluke. The fruit was sent to preserve works in the parish. The only surviving one of these is R. & W. Scott in Clyde Street.

FRUIT PICKERS AT WORK in a strawberry garden. Though the scene looks idyllic enough, the work was back-breaking. Notice the thatched cottage behind. Compare the women's headgear with that on p. 151.

THE DRILL HALL IN MARKET ROAD was built by public subscription for the Lanarkshire Yeomanry in memory of the men who lost their lives in the Boer War.

THE EARLIEST KNOWN CHURCH in the parish was Forest Kirk, an early religious settlement on the banks of the Clyde. When it was abandoned at an unknown date, Carluke Kirk was built. In 1715 the bell-tower in this photograph was erected.

CHILDREN from the orthopaedic and tuberculosis wards at Law Hospital out for a breath of fresh air, in about 1949. Modern drugs have virtually eliminated tuberculosis.

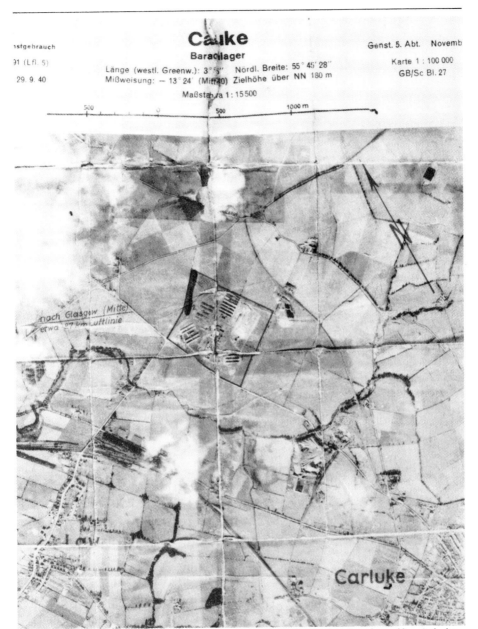

Cauke

Baracßlager

Länge (westl. Greenw.): 3° ß''   Nördl. Breite: 55° 45' 28''
Mißweisung: – 13° 24' (Mitte0) Zielhöhe über NN 180 m

Maßstab a 1 : 15 500

1stgebrauch

31 (Lfl. 5)

29. 9. 40

Genst. 5. Abt.   Novemb

Karte 1 : 100 000

GB/Sc Bl. 27

500   0   500   1000 m

nach Glasgow (Mitte)
etwa ~7 km Luftlinie

Carluke

LUFTWAFFE AERIAL RECONNAISSANCE PHOTOGRAPH of Carluke showing Law Hospital. Law Hospital was the first of Scotland's Emergency Medical Service Hospitals, built in only a few months in 1939. The photograph shows that the Germans thought the hospital was a barracks. Though originally intended to last only a few years, 'The Law' is still the district's general hospital.

MAULDSLIE CASTLE was built in the 1790s by the 5th Earl of Hyndford, to a design by Adam. Though not completed until 1890, the castle was demolished in the 1930s, the then owner being unable to maintain it. The impressive gatehouse still stands on the Clyde Valley road. In July 1914 King George V and Queen Mary were guests of James Hozier, Lord Newlands, who then owned the castle; schoolchildren lined the roads and the Lanarkshire Yeomanry provided the guard of honour.

MILTON LOCKHART was built in 1829 in the Scottish baronial style by William Lockart, MP for the County. The site was chosen by Sir Walter Scott, and the library was a replica of Scott's own library in his house at Abbotsford. In the 1980s a Japanese businessman transported the building stone by stone to Japan, to rebuild it as a major tourist attraction.

CROSSFORD VILLAGE. The turning to the left goes over the bridge pictured on p. 36. The imposing house at the end is Drumassie, built by John Leiper, baker in the village, in 1903.

LANARK ROAD, CROSSFORD, looking from the Tillietudlem Hotel.

WALTER SCOTT'S TILLIETUDLEM CASTLE was supposed to have been modelled on the nearby Craignethan Castle. The Tillietudlem Hotel took its name from Scott's creation. The dormer windows are typically bayed.

ROSEBANK, the last of the picturesque Clyde Valley villages, actually strays into the parish of Dalserf. It was built to house the estate workers of Lord Newlands. The Popinjay Hotel on the right is reputedly built on the site of an archery contest described by Sir Walter Scott in his *Old Mortality*, the 'popping jay' being an archery target. A 'Wappenschaw' shoot is regularly held nearby.

CARFIN HOUSE has disappeared, although the coach house still remains. Today it is used as a garden and craft centre.

HAZELBANK, another of the Clyde Valley villages, in about 1900. The buildings look much the same today, though the post office on the left is now a private house. In the summer the beautifully cultivated raised gardens on the right make this a most attractive village.

Carstairs, Carnwath and District

NEWBIGGING'S UNOBTRUSIVE GARAGE in the 1940s.

NEWBIGGING in about 1910, with the school in the middle distance. Even then unsympathetic buildings (such as the brick dwelling on the right) could clash with the stone and thatch around them.

THE UNUSUAL CORINTHIAN COLUMN of Newbigging's mercat cross with the school behind.

THE VILLAGE OF TARBRAX grew up (and all but died) around the short-lived oil shale industry. Preston Smith, proprietor of the Tarbrax service station, offered cottage teas at 1s., high teas at 1s. 6d. and 2s., and the facility of a 'retiring room', in rather cosier surroundings than today's service stations.

THE RATHER STRANGELY NAMED PLEASANCE at Wilsontown in around 1904. Wilsontown had risen and fallen as an iron town in the nineteenth century, and waxed and waned with the coal industry in the twentieth.

Wilsontown, Station

WILSONTOWN was built for the workers in one of Scotland's early ironworks, started by the Wilson brothers in 1799. It was the principal village in the area and attracted the railway, while the nearby and now much larger village of Forth never had passenger services.

THE MAIN STREET IN FORTH in about 1910.

ALL THINGS TO ALL MEN (AND WOMEN) in Forth and the surrounding district, the Stark family had things sewn up!

AUCHENGRAY PARISH CHURCH & SCHOOL.

AUCHENGRAY SCHOOLCHILDREN line up for a photograph in about 1908. Hillhead farm is in the left background.

AUCHENGRAY VILLAGE before the Great War. Mid Auchengray farm is on the left. The horse and cart stand in front of a very unobtrusive pub.

LIBBERTON VILLAGE in about 1907, showing typical corn stooks. Barley has largely replaced oats as the main cereal crop.

ORIGINALLY COUTHALLY LOCH, the White Loch supplied fish and fowl for the Sommerville's noble table. It provided some recreation for locals in the form of curling and boating, but sand and gravel quarrying has reduced what was a 25-acre lake to a shadow of its former self.

ALL THAT REMAINED in 1902 of Couthally Castle, the seat of the once powerful Sommerville family of Carnwath.

JAMES WILLIAMSON, deputy Lieutenant of Lanarkshire, deputy Grand Master of Upper Ward in about 1912.

THE CROSS AT CARNWATH, erected in 1516. The distances from Edinburgh to Ayr and from Peebles to Glasgow via various villages (including Carnwath) are marked on the shaft. The urn on the top blew off in 1962 but was replaced in the early '70s.

CARNWATH, TOWNFOOT, in about 1911. The post cart is on the left. Behind is one of those new-fangled cars, perhaps about to replace the horse cabs hired out by Mr Robertson on the right.

CARNWATH in about 1910. Mrs Brockie, who ran a well-known tea room, is conscientiously sweeping the cobbles. The novelist John Buchan describes having a ham and egg tea there.

ONE OF THE CARNWATH VILLAGE PUMPS in use about the turn of the century.

CARNWATH STATION was opened in 1848 rather inconveniently far from the village, a fact which contributed to its closure in 1966. In 1903 a slaughter house, the building on the left, was erected by W. & R. Jackson.

MRS BERTRAM OF KERSEWELL funded a soup kitchen for the poor of the parish in the early 1880s, a venture necessitated by the failure of the Wilsontown ironworks. The worthy folk who carried out the enterprise are pictured here in front of 111–113 Main Street in about 1882.

THE LAMPITS FLOAT FERRY over the Clyde between Carnwath and Pettinain commenced in about 1829. A float ferry is a shallow draught vessel pulled by chains winched on board. Here we see it in about 1900, with ferryman Andrew Cullen's daughter operating the winch.

ANOTHER VIEW OF THE LAMPITS FERRY carrying Andrew Smith's baker's van. Smith's still sell their wares all over the district by van – motorized of course. Notice the beautifully constructed hay stack in the background, on stilts to preserve it should the river flood.

THE OLD JAIL AT CARNWATH was established in 1530 as a court of justice. It was renovated in 1705 as a tollbooth, the cells remaining. In 1874 it was replaced and used instead as a shop before its demolition in 1929.

MASS PRODUCTION of cotton and linen cloth had put many hand spinners and weavers out of business, but there was still a need for the quality cloth which could be produced by hand. Mr and Mrs Hugh Kelly, pictured here, had their workshop in their house in South Back Road, Carnwath.

PETTINAIN around the turn of the century. Although the site of an ancient settlement, Pettinain has remained a very small rural community.

PETTINAIN seen from the other end of the main street – probably on the same day as the previous shot.

ANNIE LAURIE, who lived at the top of the brae in Pettinain. She is working a single drive Shetland traveller.

FLOOD AT CARSTAIRS AUG R 1915   A.BROWN&Co No 2

THE NEWSPAPERS report that it was unusually heavy, localized rainfall that caused the entensive flooding at Carstairs Junction on 2 August 1915. Brown's photographers lost no time in recording the event.

THESE TWO SEEM QUITE PLEASED about the flood, which can only have added to the difficulties of wartime. Is the man upstairs actually fishing?

THE RAILWAY SIDINGS were quite extensively damaged by the flood waters. Posing amid the ruins is Charlie Howland.

CLYDE VIEW, CARSTAIRS JUNCTION in 1917. This depressing row of railway houses has now gone.

CARSTAIRS JUNCTION in about 1920, showing the railway yard. As always the children gather wherever the photographer goes.

A REMARKABLE SERIES OF PHOTOGRAPHS showing the arched stone road bridge over the main line at Carstairs Junction being replaced by a girder bridge to give more clearance to the trains, though it did little to improve the approach to the station for road traffic.

BRICK AND METAL replace the traditional stonework.

TEA LADIES at Carstairs Junction railway station. Nearest the camera is Jean Adam.

CARSTAIRS JUNCTION BOY SCOUT PIPE BAND in the 1920s. Back row, left to right: W. Carruthers, Neil, Campbell, W. Cooper, T. Robertson. Front row: Greenshields, A. Adam, B. Cooper.

Douglas and District

DOUGLAS WATER COLLIERY in about 1940. Colliers were employed mainly from the villages of Ponfeigh and Rigside. The colliery operated for several decades, even in the depression years of the 1930s, due to the demand for its fine quality coal. It closed in the 1960s.

UNDERGROUND AT DOUGLAS WATER COLLIERY in 1940. A rare photograph of underground 'hewers' and 'drawers', in shirts or 'semmits', moleskin trousers and tackety boots.

DOUGLAS CASTLE in 1900, photographed from the other side of the lake. This was the main domicile of the Earls of Home, the other being at The Hirsel, Coldstream. The castle was demolished in the 1920s, being undermined by the extraction of coal from the Earl's own collieries.

FOG HOUSE, DOUGLAS, in the Windrow Wood and Glen. This area was opened up for unemployed weavers to construct paths and a carriageway. The Fog House was a rest shelter, so called because in time it was covered with moss or 'fog'.

DOUGLAS CASTLE in 1900, viewed from the front of the ornamental gardens.

THE RUIN OF DOUGLAS CASTLE, built in 1475 and accidentally burnt in 1758. It was immortalized by Walter Scott in his novel *Castle Dangerous*.

ORNAMENTAL GATE with shapes of garden implements (made by a blacksmith) which was in the grounds of Douglas Castle. Since the demolition of the castle, the gate has been preserved at Castlemains, Douglas, another residence of the Home family.

MONKS FOOT GLEN in Douglas parish. The Monkswater flows through the glen which is named after the use made of paths in the area by monks who travelled from Melrose.

THE ESTATE OF DOUGLAS CASTLE was, and still is, famed for its fine breed of Highland cattle. 'Jock' is the one on the left.

DOUGLAS MAIN STREET in about 1900. Douglas is now a conservation village, too late unfortunately to save many of its oldest buildings which were demolished in the 1960s.

DOUGLAS MAIN STREET in 1910. Many of the shops in the centre of Douglas have closed because residents are able to travel to larger shopping centres in nearby towns by car.

DOUGLAS MAIN STREET in 1930. A typical street in the village centre, with roads that cars have to negotiate slowly, and narrow pavements.

THE WEST GATE AT DOUGLAS CASTLE in about 1906, showing thatched cottages. One of the women in the doorway is holding a baby in a blanket shawl or plaid.

FERNIHAUGH FARM at Dolphinton in 1915 showing neat, skilfully made cornstacks, and Ayrshire cattle.

ST BRIDE'S CHURCH, DOUGLAS. A place of worship has stood on this site since around 1150. The building has tombs and relics concerning the Douglas family and battle flags associated with the Cameronian regiment. On one side of the church is the oldest public clock in Scotland, dating from 1565.

A MONUMENT TO JAMES, EARL OF ANGUS. The Cameronian regiment, named after a prominent Covenanter, Richard Cameron, was raised in Douglas on 14 May 1689, as the 'killing times' drew to a close. It was disbanded in 1968.

DOUGLAS. 1914. The funeral cortège of the Earl of Home on its way to the interment in Douglas New Cemetery.

YEOMANRY CAMP in about 1900 at the bridge on the road to Douglas West, where there was a shooting range. The volunteer soldiers (the equivalent of today's Territorial Army) were billeted in tents and the horses in temporary buildings shown on the right of the picture.

Lanark, New Lanark and Kirkfieldbank

THIS LOVELY VICTORIAN BUILDING with fine stonework and crow-stepped gables was the post office in Lanark until shortly after the Second World War.

High Street, Lanark

THE HIGH STREET looking from the Cross in 1910. Until about 1834 the Puddin' Burn ran down what is now the High Street. Henry Craig, the chemist, was taken over by Boots in the 1950s, but there is still a Stead and Simpson shoe shop, although it is further up the High Street.

JACK'S THE IRONMONGERS, a long-established business in the building which had housed the post office in the nineteenth century. The delivery boy would have had a hard time pedalling that bike up and down Lanark's hilly streets.

THE WELLGATE in about 1906. On the right is the Black Bull Hotel with its sign for the Scottish Cyclists' Union. Lanark was a favourite venue for cyclists in those days. When the hotel was demolished, a very old deep well was found and filled in.

LANARK has always been a military town. The Lanarkshire Imperial Yeomanry drilled at the racecourse in June or in the autumn, and then usually held a race meeting with stakes of £10 to £35. This is a camp in 1912.

ANOTHER VIEW OF THE MILITIA CAMP on Lanark Moor. The horses seem to have had better accommodation than the soldiers.

CLEARLY, FAMILIES WERE ALLOWED TO VISIT THE MILITIA CAMP.

A RECRUITMENT MARCH in Lanark by the Highland Light Infantry in 1915. 'Your King and country want you, and as the 71st, one of your county regiments, requires more men, here is your chance to take part, not only in maintaining the unbroken traditions of heroism and valour belonging to this corps, but also the British Army, of which it is no mean unit.' Who could have resisted that?

ATION GROUND, LANARK. TINTO in distance.

THE AVIATION SCHOOL was opened at Lanark in the following year by Major William Hugh Ewan. A hangar was built for him at the racecourse by Purdie of Lanark. J.A. Drexel, pictured here, set a new world record for altitude at 6,750 ft.

THE SCOTTISH INTERNATIONAL AVIATION MEETING took place at Lanark in 1910 and drew huge crowds. The Racecourse railway station was built to cope with transport problems. Famous aviators from Britain, America and Europe competed for prizes and broke several flying records.

THE LANARK MILITARY BAND which made its first appearance in the Templars Hall on 3 April 1903. It is clearly well equipped, though unlikely to do much marching with double basses.

LANARK GOLF CLUB was founded in 1851 and claims to be the seventeenth oldest in Britain. This shows the club house with a view of the loch and Tinto hill in about 1930.

THE ANCIENT CELEBRATION OF LANIMERS takes place every year in June when the old Burgh boundaries (landmarches) are checked. A full week of festivities is enjoyed by Lanarkians from far and near. On the Thursday morning there is a procession of decorated floats, bands and the crowning of the Lanimer Queen. This photograph is of Lanimer morning in 1872. In those days there was no queen, just a procession of the civic dignitaries of the town.

THE CROWNING OF THE FIRST LANIMER QUEEN in front of the old cross in 1893.

WALLACE GAINED FREEDOM FOR YOUR FOREFATHERS
BRITONS, KEEP IT FOR YOUR CHILDREN.

LANIMER DAY was still celebrated during the First World War, and the statue of Wallace was decorated with a suitably nationalistic slogan.

A FLOAT from the 1915 procession, 'Moonbeams'.

THE CROWNING CEREMONY in 1917, looking more as it does today, in front of St Nicholas' church. The old cross has gone and a special platform has been built.

THE LANIMER QUEEN of 1919, Miss Margaret Clarkson of Kirkfieldbank, is crowned, not in front of St Nicholas' church as usual, but in front of the Co-op building on the south side of the High Street.

THE PROCESSION of 1919 included this patriotic float.

The Lanimer Queen's Reception and Dance
. . 1927 . .

PROGRAMME

Selection: Orchestra

Entrance of Lanimer Queen

National Anthem

Entrance of Characters

*Presentation of Bangle
to Lanimer Queen*
By Mrs ALSTON

Court Dance: Triumph

Song: De Old Banjo: Brownies

Tableau Vivante: A Fairy Waxwork

Team Dance: Speed The Plough

Song and Dance by Sylvan Fairies

Supper in Camp: Girl Guides

Display by 1st Lanark Boys' Brigade

Song by the Waxwork Fairies

Dutch Dance

Rhymes by the Brownies

Sea Shanties: Bobby Shafto
When Johnny comes down to Hilo
1st Lanark Life Boys

Court Dance: Lady Coventry's Reel

Song and Dance: Happy Hours

Quartet and Dance by the Waxwork
Fairies

Dance: Passing of Time

Team Dance: Soldiers' Joy

Display by 1st Lanark Boys' Brigade

Spanish Dance

Sea Shanties: Elsie Marley
Billy Boy
1st Lanark Life Boys

Auld Lang Syne

THE RECEPTION AND DANCE PROGRAMME of 1927.

LANIMERS, 1922. A traditional float – 'The raggle taggle gypsies'.

ALL THE IMPORTANT EVENTS in the town took place in front of the church at the cross. This is the official proclamation of the accession of King George V in 1910. Notice how everybody in the crowd wore hats or bunnets.

THE LAKE PAVILION AT LANARK LOCH, 1907. The loch was created from a swamp in about 1850, and has provided recreation for Lanarkians ever since. With the advent of the motor car people came from much farther afield to enjoy the amenities at the loch.

SOME EDWARDIAN LADIES enjoying a trip in the little steamer on the loch in 1908.

LANARK CROSS in about 1905. St Nicholas' church was built in 1777 and replaced St Kentigern's as the parish church. The bell is much older, being dated 1110, and the steeple bears the inscription 'I did for twice three centuries hing, and into Lanark city ring'. On the left of the picture is part of the old tollbooth which was built in the eighteenth century.

A SLIGHTLY LATER VIEW OF LANARK CROSS. The railings are still in front of the church but the old cross has gone.

BANNATYNE STREET in 1908, with two carriages and wide pavements. It seems narrower today although the buildings are much the same. The Royal Oak Hotel was then the Victoria Station Hotel.

BANNATYNE STREET a few years later (c. 1913). The hotel has become Nicholl's Station Hotel but the street still looks broad enough.

STATION SQUARE in the late 1930s. Just visible on the right is St Leonard's church, now demolished. The Royal Oak Hotel then had petrol pumps on the pavement outside. There were plenty of hotels in Lanark to cater for the large numbers of tourists who came to the Falls of Clyde.

WESTPORT, looking up towards the Bloomgate. This was one of the four gates into the medieval town, demolished in the eighteenth century.

A BUSY SCENE IN NEW LANARK. The mills were built by Richard Arkwright and David Dale between 1788 and 1826. Dale's son-in-law, Robert Owen, made the village world famous through his treatment of workers and their families. He built homes and a co-operative store and encouraged them to improve themselves through education.

VILLAGERS OF NEW LANARK in about 1890. The village has been restored and the buildings are recognizable today, but when did you last see a girr and cleek (a metal hoop and hooked stick) or washing hanging from a window? The semicircular building in the middle distance is the Counting House, from where the workers were paid.

THE VILLAGE STORE with staff posing proudly outside. Their customers would be the mill workers. Dale had introduced the token system for goods from the shop, a system which was abused by the mill owners in the north of England. The last mill in New Lanark closed in 1968.

A MILK CART in about 1920, but taking the post round as well.

THE GOUROCK ROPEWORKS COMPANY were major employers in Lanark and New Lanark. This is one of their steam-driven Foden lorries in about 1905.

G.H. GREENHOUGH was a well-known travelling evangelist in the area. Here he is pictured with his mission van in New Lanark where he would have held outdoor meetings, accompanying the Moody and Sankey hymns on his concertina.

CLEGHORN MILL. This cornmill has stood since the seventeenth century. A Roman road forded the river near here.

A PANORAMIC VIEW OF KIRKFIELDBANK taken from high up the Lanark Brae. The single-file seventeenth-century Clydesholme Bridge was the only crossing over the Clyde on this major route as late as the 1950s, when this photograph was taken.

LINNEVILLE, KIRKFIELDBANK, looking uphill from Dublin Burn.

MOUSEMILL in about 1936. This was one of the old town mills to which the people of Lanark took (indeed in early times, *had* to take) their corn to be ground. The river that provided the power is the Mouse. The house identified in the picture as the mill is now called Mousemill House, the building in the foreground is Sorisdale.

A RICK LIFTER photographed at Linnmill, Kirkfieldbank. Linnmill used to be the home of the well known author Robert McLellan.

THESE COTTAGES IN KIRKFIELDBANK, seen here in 1909, housed a community of Irish weavers, and became known as Dublin. The burn which runs into the Clyde here is still called Dublin Burn.

STONEBYRES HOUSE, one of many mansion houses around Lanark. It was much restored and added to in the nineteenth century, and was considered to be the oldest inhabited house in Lanarkshire. It was demolished in 1934, and the estate sold off as smallholdings.

THE CLYDE falls steeply as it passes through Upper Ward and provides the site for two hydroelectric power stations. That at Stonebyres was opened in 1927.

Abington
and Leadhills

MAIN STREET IN LEADHILLS, 1914. One of the highest villages in Scotland (1,350 ft), Leadhills was the centre for mining gold and silver as well as lead. The village is also the home of the oldest subscription library in Britain, founded in 1741 as the Leadhills Miners' Reading Society and later named for Allan Ramsay the poet, perhaps Leadhills' most famous son.

LEADHILLS VILLAGE in about 1908. The postcard this is taken from carries the message, 'The pure mountain air and the charming situation of Leadhills attract visitors from far and near.'

LEADHILLS in 1933, showing the war memorial and hotel. Notice the small artillery piece on the left.

THE PRINCE OF WALES visited Leadhills and Abington in 1903 (or 1904) to stay with the Colebrook family and this is his open carriage. Gold mined at Leadhills was used in the Scottish crown jewels.

THE CURFEW BELL at Leadhills dates from 1770 when it was rung to indicate the changing shifts in the mines or gather search parties for those lost on the Lowthers, and tolled at funerals. Today it is only used to ring in the new year.

ABINGTON was a coaching village on the Glasgow–Carlisle road. In the nineteenth century it was rebuilt as an estate village by Sir Thomas Colebrooke. This shows the ivy-clad Abington Hotel with early motor cars and bike at the door. The future Napoleon III (when in exile) is reputed to have stayed here in 1839 on his way to Edinburgh.

GLENGONNAR RESIDENTIAL CAMP IN ABINGTON was built in 1940 and evacuees were housed there during the Second World War. Princess Juliana spent a night here with a group of Dutch refugees; more Dutch children came after the Nazi occupation of their country.

THE BOARDING HOUSE AT ELVANFOOT in 1904. The coming of the railways meant that people were able to get to more remote places. Elvanfoot had a reputation as a health resort and, like Leadhills and Abington, advertised the 'bracing' air.

CRAWFORD had always been a convenient stopping-off place on the road south from Glasgow until the motorway was built. This picture, dated 1904, shows the main road when there was very little motorized traffic: the water pump is still very much in evidence, and though there are plenty of telegraph wires there is as yet no street lighting.

CRAWFORD in 1915. A close-up of the imposing house just seen on the left of the previous picture. An automobile now shares the road with a horse and cart, and a wee boy plays with his girr and cleek.

TOWNFOOT, CRAWFORD. The hills rise steeply from the river and small hayfield beyond. Have the three visitors arrived in the open-topped tourer and been for a picnic?

A PEACEFUL RURAL SCENE AT CRAWFORD showing the hotel with the war memorial beyond.

THE MILL AT CRAWFORD with the wheel spectacularly in action.

AN ARTISTIC SHOT of the crossroads at Crawfordjohn in the winter of 1920.

Lesmahagow and District

A PANORAMIC VIEW of Lesmahagow from the east in about 1910.

TURFHOLM, LESMAHAGOW in about 1910. This photograph was taken from the Turfholm bridge which straddles the River Nethan at the south end of the village. On the left is Turfholm girls' public school, fronted by railings. To the right is Granny Gibson's shop, a popular haunt of schoolchildren looking for a ha'pennyworth of sweets or broken biscuits.

LESMAHAGOW PARISH CHURCH AND CHURCH SQUARE in about 1919. The church was built in 1803 on the site of a twelfth-century priory church founded by David I. The outer buildings of the priory which lay adjacent to the church were excavated during 1978/9 and are now preserved. The churchyard holds the remains of local Covenanters who were persecuted for their faith in the seventeenth century.

COALBURN AND DISTRICT COOPERATIVE SOCIETY GROCERY DEPARTMENT in Abbeygreen in about 1910. This shop is now the Gospel Hall.

THE SOUTH END OF LESMAHAGOW MAIN STREET or Abbeygreen in about 1960. The Ritz cinema and the Glebe cinema were popular until the coming of television. Despite their proprietors' efforts to maintain operation, both were eventually closed. The Ritz lay empty for many years and was demolished, together with the buildings in the foreground, in the early 1980s.

GATESIDE in about 1900, approximately one mile south of Lesmahagow. Nothing remains of the hamlet today, the area being planted with local authority housing during the 1970s – an individual community lost forever.

THE MACKIRDY FOUNTAIN in about 1910. It was erected at the junction of Abbeygreen and the New Trows Road (or Peasehill) by William Augustas Scott MacKirdy in the late 1880s. It was removed around 1926 because of the introduction of omnibuses. This being the terminus, the buses had difficulty in turning, and it was decided that the fountain be removed and re-erected in MacKirdy Park. During its demolition however, it was damaged to such an extent that it was impossible to have it resited. This junction is still referred to as 'The Fountain', although no trace of it remains.

SPRINGBANK (now New Trows Road) in about 1928, Part of the expansion of the village of Lesmahagow during the late nineteenth century. The houses and valley opposite were known as 'The Mutton Hole', which probably derived from stolen sheep being hidden in the valley after a rieving expedition, or perhaps from an area which was always used as a sheep run to the village.

NEW ROAD, Lesmahagow in about 1920. With land for building restricted in Lesmahagow village, new houses were built to the west of the village which, as it gew, became known locally as the 'New Toon'. Despite the caption on the photograph, this is not Turfholm.

Broompark, Lesmahagow

BROOMPARK in about 1924. A later extension to the village of Lesmahagow, the first house being built in about 1902. The building left of centre in the background is the New Primary School, now Milton Primary, but generally known as The White School.

LESMAHAGOW MAIN STREET or Abbeygreen in about 1920. Stodart's Royal Hotel on the left stood empty for many years before being replaced by the new public library in 1980. Nearly all the other buildings exist today. The Commercial Hotel has since taken the name Craignethan Hotel.

ABBEYGREEN in about 1897, looking south. The Royal Hotel on the right was then under the ownership of a Mr Ratho. Notice the mounting stone (bottom right).

PART OF NEW TROWS ROAD, Lesmahagow in around 1910, earlier known as Causewayfoot. The three double-storey buildings on the left are now replaced with one bungalow.

GLEBE BUILDINGS, Abbeygreen in about 1905. Construction of these buildings began on church land during the 1890s, and a housing development to the rear of these shops and flats was considered at the time, but abandoned. The overall appearance of the building has not changed over the years although the shop-fronts have been adapted to suit various needs.

TWO VIEWS OF THE MAIN STREET IN LESMAHAGOW after a flash flood on 13 July 1927, due to torrential rain lasting only one and a half hours. The Turfholm bridge over the river Nethan could not take such a volume of water and its only natural course was to flood the main street, bringing with it portions of the Sandknowe bridge, which was virtually destroyed, and huge boulders from the river bed. At its height the water level was nearly three feet.

JOHN DODDS, blacksmith in Bereholm, Lesmahagow, one of the oldest residents, planting a tree in MacKirdy Public Park in about 1937.

MILTON QUARRY, Lesmahagow in about 1900, showing a steam engine employed during the laying of the railway from Strathaven to Coalburn.

EXCAVATION NEAR LESMAHAGOW in about 1900 for the new railway track. The steam engine was given the nickname 'The Navvie'.

MEMBERS OF LESMAHAGOW BOWLING CLUB witnessing a 'measure' in about 1930.

THE BOWLING CLUB in about 1920. Members take a breather for the camera.

SEVEN PENNY FARTHINGS = 8¾d. Members of Lesmahagow Cycling Club before 1900. Left to right: ? Brown, John Brown, Tom Walker, ? Pate, William Walker, ? Walker. The central rider carried a little horn.

GREAT EXCITEMENT BRINGS THE VILLAGERS OUT to witness the new fire engine at work. The crowd that came to see the fire was so great that it was not possible for the photographer to capture the engine on film; only the water pump drawing water from the Milton Mill lake can be seen!

A BETTER VIEW OF THE FIRST FIRE ENGINE AND CREW in about 1910. It was provided by Elliot MacKirdy of Birkwood (standing in front of the engine). When Birkwood House was sold to the County Council in 1923, it was a condition of sale that the fire engine be included in the price offered.

LESMAHAGOW AMBULANCE BRIGADE in rehearsal for any eventuality during the First World War.

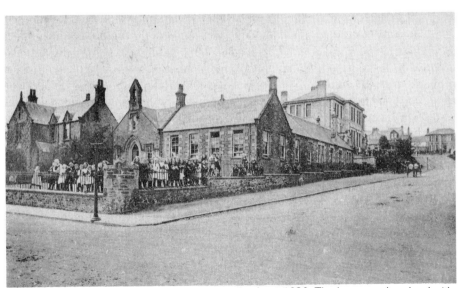

LESMAHAGOW LOWER AND HIGHER GRADE SCHOOLS in about 1920. The lower grade school with the bell-tower in the foreground was the original boys' public school built in 1872. Notice the milk cart on the right.

ALL THE FUN OF THE FAIR. A rare photograph of 'The Shows' in Lesmahagow, 1906. The family who brought the fair remained and became cinema proprietors.

LESMAHAGOW RAILWAY VIADUCT over the river Nethan in about 1910. The viaduct was demolished during the early 1980s.

LESMAHAGOW RAILWAY STATION, viaduct and 'Lye' (shunting yard for goods wagons) taken in about 1905. All evidence of the existence of the railway has now gone; the site holds a new housing development and an extension to Lesmahagow High School.

New Station, Lesmahagow.

THE NEW STATION, Lesmahagow, opened in 1904, closed in 1966.

THE MOUND, a continuation of New Trows Road, Lesmahagow in about 1910. The only building remaining is the one facing with the porch. Local authority housing has replaced some of the houses on the left.

BIRKWOOD HOUSE OR CASTLE in about 1900. Built and extended during the 1800s, it was the home of the MacKirdy family until 1920. In 1923 the house and grounds were bought by Lanark County Council for £10,000, for use as accommodation for the mentally handicapped. The hospital now houses over 200 residents.

WASHING DAY in Church Square, Lesmahagow in about 1930.

TAKING A BREAK FROM THE LAST. Francis Brown's cobblers shop in Abbeygreen in about 1920.

NETHAN VALLEY PIPE BAND in about 1948. This band had many successes during the 1940s and '50s, but was disbanded during the '60s.

BIRKWOOD GLEN, LESMAHAGOW. The reason for this gathering is not known, but is thought to be a local cattle show at the turn of the century.

EASTWOOD FARM, Lesmahagow, 1940. A land girl attends to her horses.

UP TO DATE in the fleshing trade, c. 1930.

PARKS' GARAGE, Lesmahagow, on the Glasgow–Carlisle road (A74) in 1930. Although the garage has gone, the bend in the road at that point is still referred to as Parks' corner.

BSA SIDECAR COMBINATION, a popular form of transport in the 1930s.

THE 'JULIAN BUS', a lorry run by McRae & Haldane's which converted to an omnibus when required for outings, c. 1920. There are thirty-nine on board!

A PONY AND TRAP at Auchlochan House near Lesmahagow. Shetland ponies were bred here by Charles Douglas, MP for Coatbridge during the 1920s. The 'Big House' seen in the background is, like a number of mansions in the area, now a nursing home.

THE STAFF OF MCRAE & HALDANE'S, garage and coach builders in Lesmahagow — a grim lot! The blacksmith's trade is still important in the early days of motoring.

PATHFOOT SMIDDY, Milton (Lesmahagow) in about 1910. The smiddy was situated on the old coaching road from Glasgow to the south. It has been replaced by two modern bungalows.

A FLATTERING VIEW of the 'knitwear' factory built at Turfholm in Lesmahagow in the 1950s. The Nethan Water divides it from MacKirdy Park.

CORONATION DAY, 1953. Part of the procession of decorated floats through Lesmahagow (1st Ranger Company).

THE OLD FASHIONED SWEETIE SHOP at Lintfieldbank near Coalburn in about 1920. It may be assumed that the children, especially the shoeless one, could only afford to window shop.

COALBURN STATION in about 1900, a reminder of an era which disappeared with the Beeching axe of the 1960s.

A PADDLE IN THE SEA. A group of Coalburn people on an 'away day' in about 1930.

MEMBERS OF THE COALBURN WRI at the seaside in the 1930s. Careful ladies, your slips are showing.

LIME ROW, COALBURN in 1930. The butts collected water though there was a pump in the street.

A COMMON SCENE AT A COALBURN PIT, c. 1930.

A BEVY OF COALBURN BEAUTIES putting on the style in about 1930. Left to right: Jean Simpson, Mima Pearson, Kate Mochrie, Ria Shankley, Mrs Perrie, Matt Wilson.

A RARE PHOTOGRAPH OF AUCHENHEG PIT NEAR COALBURN in about 1902. This was the bread, and not much butter, for many families in the district. Alas, the scene is no more.

THE MINERS' STRIKE of 1921. A familiar sight during those dark times: men of principle living off the charity of the soup kitchen.

COALBURN ROAD, Coalburn in about 1900. Typical miners' rows, some of which survived into the 1960s, now replaced with local authority 'all electric' houses and flats.

COALBURN INN around 1900, with 'The Maid' or No. 1 pit in the background. The shop right of centre is now demolished.

A WELCOME BREAK from the dark and the dampness for these two Coalburn miners, Andrew Brown and Tam Findlay.

OUTSIDE JAMES ADAM'S POST OFFICE in Coalburn around the turn of the century – the halcyon days of horse and carriage.

COALBURN POST OFFICE in about 1940, and we have entered the era of the automobile.

BAKER'S VAN FROM LESMAHAGOW delivering up at Coalburn in the '30s, when bread was unsliced and plastic carrier bags were unheard of.

BRAEFOOT, near Coalburn, 1930. Horse and driver (Jimmy Lockhart) 'haen a wee blaw'.

COALBURN AND DISTRICT BRASS BAND in about 1902. A popular pastime in Scottish as in English mining communities, continued today by the Coalburn Silver Band.

THE TELEGRAPH BOY outside the Coalburn post office in about 1920.

'WHA' SAW THE TATTIE HOWKERS'. A group of Coalburn children employed to pick potatoes in about 1930. 'It micht be sair oan the back, bit it's better than the schule.' Notice the bare feet.

MORE WORK ON THE UBIQUITOUS STRAWBERRY BEDS. Weeding on a plot by the back road between Kirkmuirhill and Lesmahagow in the 1930s.

DUNDUFF QUARRY near Boghead in about 1900. Much of the stone used in the foundations of the new railway through Lesmahagow at the turn of the century came from this quarry. Many of those who worked there were itinerant Irishmen.

LABOURERS AND EQUIPMENT AT DUNDUFF QUARRY, Boghead in 1900.

THE SQUARE, Auchenheath in about 1920. A rare photograph of this hamlet some two miles from Kirkmuirhill. This scene is no more.

'HAMMY' JACKSON'S BUS in about 1950. Hamilton Jackson, a bus proprietor from Auchenheath, ran a public bus service from Lanark to Lesmahagow for many years. He was very popular with his passengers – 'Hammy never let you down.'

JAMES WHYTE delivering milk for Hugh Russell's dairy in Kirkmuirhill. His float proudly proclaims that the milk is from a 'tubercle free herd', though the method of delivery hasn't changed for a century.

A SAWMILL IN KIRKMUIRHILL dealing with beech trees. The single horse pulls a huge load. This yard was believed to have been situated on the Lesmahagow–Kirkmuirhill Road.

SMIDDY AT KIRKMUIRHILL. Already the motor car impinges on his traditional business – note the primitive petrol pump on the right. The smith is Joe McRae, father of the well known rally driver Jimmy McRae.

ON THE FACE OF IT, HARD TIMES IN KIRKMUIRHILL in about 1900; but, if the faces of the women look worn, the children are well fed, well shod and warmly clothed.

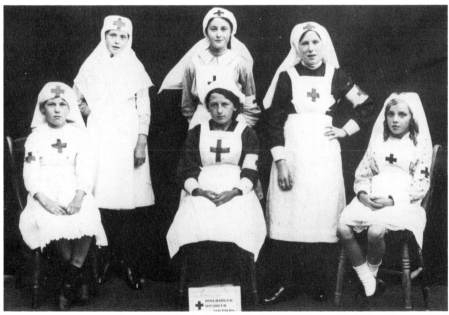

FUND RAISING was as much a part of life during the First World War as it is today. The pupils of Blackwood school, dressed as VADs, raised money for 'discharged, disabled soldiers'.

A STURDY AND APPARENTLY SUCCESSFUL FOOTBALL TEAM from Blackwood in 1912.

AGNES HAMILTON AND BARBARA WADDEL on Carlisle Road, Kurkmuirhill. The manse is in the background.

BLACKWOOD was the largest estate in Lesmahagow parish. Once the seat of the Hope Veres, the vestiges of Blackwood House can still be seen in the grounds of its modern replacement.

COOKERY CLASS AT BLACKWOOD SCHOOL, 5 June 1913. Judging by the blackboard the girls are making sago pudding.

CLASSES FROM BLACKWOOD PRIMARY SCHOOL in 1906 and 1940.